T0078431

Living in His Wisdom

Acronym of the Word Wisdom as Revealed in Scripture

ELISHA T. KODUA

WESTBOW
PRESS®
A DIVISION OF THOMAS NELSON
& ZONDERVAN

WestBow Press books may be ordered through booksellers or by contacting:

WestBow Press
A Division of Thomas Nelson & Zondervan
1663 Liberty Drive
Bloomington, IN 47403
www.westbowpress.com
844-714-3454

Scripture taken from the King James Version of the Bible.

ISBN: 978-1-6642-1112-4 (sc)
ISBN: 978-1-6642-1114-8 (hc)
ISBN: 978-1-6642-1113-1 (e)

Library of Congress Control Number: 2020921624

Print information available on the last page.

WestBow Press rev. date: 11/10/2020

Contents

Introduction

Wisdom is the principle thing, say the sacred scriptures. For this reason, there is a need for all humankind to know and understand what wisdom is all about. It's my humble prayer that by the time you finish reading this book, the eyes of your understanding will be opened to see and to know the need to get and possess godly wisdom in all your endeavors.

My advice to you is to stay with wisdom, live in wisdom, and be controlled by the wisdom of Christ.

1

Definition of Wisdom

What does the Bible say about wisdom? Many dictionaries try to define the word, but the biblical meaning of *wisdom* stands out among all other definitions. The word *wisdom* according to the Holy Scriptures can simply be defined as the righteous use of what God has given to you or deposited in you. It means giving of your best to God through the godly use of the gifts and the talents instilled in you. It involves the application of given and acquired knowledge through the revelation of the Holy Scriptures.

Types of Wisdom

The Holy Scriptures help us understand that there are two major types of wisdom: wisdom from above (God-given wisdom) and earthly wisdom (humans' craftiness, cunning, and deception). Godly wisdom is described as God-given wisdom. It is wisdom from above because it descends from God.

The Bible tells us that such wisdom is "first pure, then peaceable, gentle, and easy to be entreated, full of mercy and good fruits, without partiality, and without hypocrisy" (James 3:17). Godly wisdom or wisdom from God is also called the "hidden wisdom," according to the epistle of Paul to the Corinthians:

> Howbeit we speak wisdom among them that are perfect: yet not the wisdom of this world, nor of the princes of this world, that come to naught: But we speak the wisdom of God in a mystery, even the hidden wisdom, which God ordained before the world unto our glory. (1 Corinthians 2:6–7)

It is called the hidden wisdom because it is hidden from the world and is revealed to all those who will come to the saving knowledge of our Lord and Savior, Jesus Christ.

Paul the apostle wrote this mystery to the Corinthian church and to everyone in all generations to reveal Christ Jesus as the hidden wisdom of God. The description of the heavenly wisdom tells us that godly wisdom is not for all people. It is a type of wisdom that is given to a category of people who are pure within and without any defilement— peaceful without any chaos and confusions, gentle without any strife, easy to be entreated, full of mercy without wickedness, godly without blasphemy, and finally, transparent without any partiality.

I pray that this type of wisdom will be your portion—and that of your family as well—as your God-given ministry in Jesus's mighty name. The Lord will continue to make you wise unto salvation through faith, which is in Christ Jesus. You will act in wisdom, you will walk in wisdom, you will proclaim His words of wisdom, and you will forever dwell in wisdom in Jesus's mighty name.

Earthly wisdom is described as earthly because heaven rejects it. It can only be operated among the ungodly people on earth. It can never be accepted in heaven. It is a cunning or deceptive way of living. It includes cheating on one another, defrauding an individual or a group of people, setting up a trap for a fellow brother or sister to fall into, conniving with others to take advantage of people, moving the pillar off the way for others to fall, and many more you can think of. The Bible describes this type of wisdom as impure and unholy. It is my humble prayer that this type of wisdom will never be your portion in Jesus's mighty name. If you have in one way or another acted or demonstrated or even found yourself in any of the characteristics of an ungodly wisdom, God will help you come out from it in Jesus's mighty name.

The Lifestyle of the Wise

E very wise person by inspiration of the Holy Ghost lives a distinctive lifestyle, which makes him or her different from others who do not possess the godly wisdom from heaven. Such people have hearts full of the Word of God, as the well is full of water. They live and reside in the center of the will of God, never deviating or turning to the right or left. They are focused and single-minded, with a single goal and pursuit.

Wise people preach like warriors. They teach the Word of God with confidence and with the unction of the Holy Spirit. They speak, exhort, and rebuke sharply with all diligence and carefulness. They never get weary. They are always on the mountaintop, a mountain of success and freedom, and never get close to the valley of sin, evil, and deceit.

They patiently wait upon the Lord before taking steps. In fact, they delight in waiting for the fulfillment of the promises of God concerning life, family, ministry, and other endeavors. They never sleep or slumber while waiting for the fulfillment of the promises of God.

Acronym of Wisdom
Revealed in Scripture

Each of the letters in the word *wisdom* carries a message and characterizes the nature and the life of Christ. This means that each of the letters in the word *wisdom* represents Christ Himself. Therefore, anyone who possesses any of the characteristics referred to in the word *wisdom* is described as a wise person. This is because possession of any one of these characteristics means possession of all the rest. In simple terms, each of the letters in the word carries the same message and meaning. It is the will of God and a prayer of the Lord Jesus Christ that the Holy Spirit will enable you to clearly understand the mysteries revealed in this book and be full of wisdom in Jesus's mighty name.

What then is wisdom? *Wisdom* means **walking in the light of God** (1 John 1:7). All wise people walk in the light. Their deeds are opened to God and to all people. They live transparent lives before God and people. They have clear consciences toward

God and toward others. They do not give room to the work of darkness; they distance themselves from every deed of darkness. Their ways are clear and embittered to darkness. They are rich in God's grace and full of confidence in God. They do not lean in the arms of humans. They show a clear picture of their savior and are the image of the only begotten Son of God, Jesus. They do not fear to be counted among those who trust in the Lord. They demonstrate true love toward God and others and walk and live their lives as the one who has called them does (1 John 2:6). Since they walk and do the deeds of the light, their actions, attitudes, and entire lives bring and draw others to the light.

They walk and live by faith in all circumstances. They never allow those who walk in the dark to influence and manipulate them. They are mindful of what they say, what they think, and what they do.

They love all people with the love of God without any hatred or bitterness (1 John 2:9–11). They simply live out the life of Christ. They act, talk, and think like Christ. They are an example to other believers in words, in conversation, in charity, in spirit, in faith, and in purity (1 Timothy 4:12).

The contrary is a foolish person. I pray you will not be considered a foolish person in Jesus's mighty name.

Wisdom means **inspiring others** through the ministrations of the Holy Spirit. Wise people make every effort to inspire and encourage other believers to remain in the Lord despite what they may be going through. They make it a daily duty to motivate others with their lifestyles, with their testimonies, and with their words. They do not discourage others. They encourage unity and discourage division and disunity. They use the sacred scriptures to motivate, exhort, rebuke, and counsel those who are weak and downtrodden. Those who draw close to wise people receive strength from the Lord. They are indeed children of an encourager. They declare the whole counsel of God to those they come across and help build up the body of Christ and stir up the gifts in other believers. They are simply like Christ.

Wisdom means **seeking and serving the Savior** first in truth and in holiness before anything else. Wise people commit all of themselves as well as all their possessions to serving the Lord. They place God in the first and foremost position in their entire lives. They never leave the house without talking to God. They never go anywhere without asking the Lord. The Lord Jesus becomes the center of their plans and decisions. They simply love God more and above anything else in life.

They pour all their hearts before the altar with true holiness and righteousness. Their righteousness exceeds that of the scribes and the Pharisees, who desire the praises of people more than of God.

They do not hold the truth in vain. They live by the truth. They dwell in truthfulness, never speaking lies. They bind themselves with the truth. No amount of money can buy the truth (which is Jesus Christ) from them.

Wisdom means **doing the will of the Father**, who is in heaven. Wise people delight in doing the will of God. They make the laws of God the priority in their lives. They have crucified self-will and have taken the will of the Father as their daily duty, weekly wages, and monthly movements.

They never take a step without hearing from God. They build their houses upon the rock, the rain will spuriously descend, the wind will vehemently blow on them, the storms will rise against them, but they shall never fall, for they are founded upon the rock of ages, the solid rock that is Jesus Christ.

They are like a tree planted by the river. They bring forth fruit in their season, their leaves shall not wither, and all they do shall prosper (Psalm 1:1–3).

They open the door of salvation to all sinners. They point the savior to others. They make the preaching of the gospel a mandate and a daily duty.

They never shut the door of salvation to sinners. They never disobey the heavenly calling or vision. They are like Paul the apostle, who was ready to be bound, beaten, and killed because of the salvation of others. He is always conscious of transforming and saving lives through the power of the gospel.

What is wisdom? *Wisdom* means **obeying the heavenly vision or calling**. The act of wisdom also has to do with obeying the call of God to Salvation, the call to sanctification and holiness of life, the call to the spirit-filled, and the call to serve.

Wise people first respond to God's call to salvation. When they hear the salvation message, they do not disregard it but rather surrender their entire lives to God through our savior Jesus Christ. They make their sins plain to God and ask for forgiveness and total cleansing and remission.

After salvation, they do not stop. They press on to the call to sanctification. They understand the need for inner cleansing and washing away of the Adamic nature. They allow the Spirit of God to operate their hearts, remove the diseases and the sicknesses of the old person, and plant in them new hearts, which desire and thirst for righteousness.

They then move on toward perfection by desiring to be empowered through the influence of the "dunamis" power of the Holy Ghost.

They understand the need to maintain the

righteousness of God through the empowerment of the Holy Spirit. Therefore, they allow the power of the Holy Spirit to work wonders in their lives. They live a spirit-controlled life. The self is crucified; the desires of the flesh are put under control. They bring every thought of evil into captivity and subject to the obedience of Christ.

They hold onto the fact that obedience to the heavenly vision is not possible without the enablement of the Spirit. No wonder Jesus, our divine teacher, asked His disciples to tarry in Jerusalem to receive the Holy Ghost before carrying out the Great Commission.

> But ye shall receive power, after that the Holy Ghost is come upon you: and ye shall be witnesses unto me both in Jerusalem, and in all Judaea, and in Samaria, and unto the uttermost part of the earth. (Acts 1:8)

However, disobedience to God's call and His Word reveals the foolishness of a person to the world. What does the term *foolishness* mean? As the opposite of wisdom, *foolishness* can be defined through the inspiration of the Holy Spirit as disobeying the ordinances of God. In other words, it is an act of doing what is contrary to the commandments of God.

Those who tend to behave foolishly are not wise because they do not have Christ. If they have Christ, they will always speak and act like Christ. In the real sense, all fools lack Christ, while all the wise like Christ. I pray you will be wise in Jesus's name.

What then is wisdom? *Wisdom* means **maintaining a constant and consistent fellowship and faithfulness** to God and humankind. Wise people are the those who always see to it that there is a constant connection between themselves and God. They do not allow the affairs of this world to disconnect them from the Almighty God. They always dwell and abide in the vine. They examine themselves on a daily basis to make sure they are still in the faith. They live and make their decisions based on the leading and guidance of the Holy

Spirit. They simply walk in the spirit and shun the lust of the flesh. They are willing to lose their lives to preserve their salvation. They never get weary because they wait on the Lord always. They look to Jesus alone to obtain help in times of need. They are not only faithful to God in all aspects of life but are found to be faithful to their fellow human beings as well.

Biblical Characters Who Demonstrated the Wisdom of God in Their Time

I t is remarkably interesting to understand that the Bible itself is a book of wisdom. It is a book full of wisdom and knowledge of our Lord and Savior Jesus Christ, who gave up Himself as a ransom for many, for all those who will believe, for the Jews first and the Gentiles.

There are so many instances in the Bible where some men and women of God demonstrated the wisdom of God in their time, and they are even more relevant to us in this generation and beyond.

Enoch

According to the sacred scriptures, Enoch was the son of Jared (Genesis 5:19–21), the father of Methuselah and the great-grandfather of Noah. He is the author of the book of Jude and was also called Enoch, the scribe of judgment.

He prophesied and told people about the coming of the Lord in His time. He lived just before the flood and after the fall of man, yet he walked with God without any backsliding. He began His walk with the Lord after his son Methuselah was born when Enoch was sixty-five years old. It was an era of unimaginable evil, yet he walked before the Lord with a perfect heart.

He maintained a consistent and unbreakable relationship with the heavenly Father. His holiness to God was above and beyond human and earthly descriptions. His entire life pleased God in such a way that God took him to heaven.

My dear reader, if Enoch was able to please God throughout his lifetime, you too can please the Lord today. By the grace of God, you too can live to please God at all times and in all places. The grace of God can keep you till Jesus comes.

God the Father can keep all His sons and daughters from falling into sin and Satan's traps. Commit all your ways into His hands, and He shall make you like Enoch in Jesus's mighty name.

Abraham

Abraham happens to be the most well-known of the biblical patriarchs. From him, all Israelites as well as the entire world derived faith; hence, he is called the Father of Faith.

God called Abraham (then Abram) out of his own country, away from his kindred, and away from his father's house into a land that God promised to show him and to give to his descendants (Genesis 12:1). God also promised to make his descendants a great nation (Genesis 12:2) in the land of Canaan.

Abram immediately obeyed the heavenly calling by taking his extended family to Canaan to live there as nomads. It is recorded in the previous chapter, Genesis 11, that *wisdom* means obeying the heavenly calling or vision. Abram demonstrated wisdom by obeying the call of God to forsake his own kindred and go to an unknown land or destination. The entire lifestyle of Abram was characterized by total obedience to God.

When the call of God came to him, he did not consider his state of life at that time. He didn't think of what would happen to his father's house; neither did he consider to where he was being called. But he saw the need to obey God first before anything else. He regarded the one who has called him to be more important to him than anything else. This was a great demonstration of the wisdom of God.

A wise man always considers the things of God as first and foremost in his life. He gives heed to the demand of God more than those of humans. Abram did not worry about the fate or the future of his father's household; he concentrated on where God was taking him.

Moreover, Abram obeyed not only the call of God for separation but also the call of God to sacrifice. God told Abram to sacrifice his only son, Isaac, to Him as a burnt offering. Let us read this to see the reality of it.

> And it came to pass after these things, that God did tempt Abraham, and said unto him, Abraham: and he said, Behold, here I am. And he said, Take now thy son, thine only son Isaac, whom thou lovest,

and get thee into the land of Moriah;
and offer him there for a burnt offering
upon one of the mountains which I will
tell thee of. (Genesis 22:1–2 KJV)

I believe Abram might not have been anticipating hearing such a thing from God, who had promised to make a great nation out of his descendants. But as a wise man and obedient servant of God, he demonstrated a prompt obedience to God. Verse 3 says,

And Abraham rose up early in the
morning, and saddled his ass, and took
two of his young men with him, and
Isaac his son, and clave the wood for the
burnt offering, and rose up, and went
unto the place of which God had told
him. (Genesis 22:3)

This is indeed a real example and demonstration of a true obedience to God. No wonder God fulfilled His plan, His purpose, and His promises concerning Abram by making him a father of all nations. His name was changed to Abraham because of his obedience to God. In Genesis 17, the Word of God says,

> And when Abram was ninety years old and nine, the Lord appeared to Abram, and said unto him, I am the Almighty God; walk before me, and be thou perfect. And I will make my covenant between thee and me and will multiply thee exceedingly. And Abram fell on his face: and God talked with him, saying, as for me, behold, my covenant is with thee, and thou shalt be a father of many nations. Neither shall thy name any more be called Abram, but thy name shall be Abraham; for a father of many nations have I made thee. And I will make thee exceeding fruitful, and I will make nations of thee, and kings shall come out of thee. And I will establish my covenant between me and thee and thy seed after thee in their generations

for an everlasting covenant, to be a God unto thee, and to thy seed after thee. And I will give unto thee, and to thy seed after thee, the land wherein thou art a stranger, all the land of Canaan, for an everlasting possession; and I will be their God. (Genesis 17:1–8)

My dear friend, in which area of life have you disobeyed God? God demands your complete obedience to Him and His Word. Make it a point from today on to obey God without questioning why or how. Decide from now on to put God first in all things, and the Lord will keep you first as well in all things in Jesus's mighty name.

Moses

Moses responded to the call of God at the age of eighty when he was taking care of the sheep belonging to his father-in-law, Jethro, the Medianite, at Mount Horeb.

The Bible tells us,

> The angel of the Lord appeared unto him in a flame of fire out of the midst of a bush: and he looked, and, behold, the bush burned with fire, and the bush was not consumed. And Moses said, I will now turn aside, and see this great sight, why the bush is not burnt. And when the Lord saw that he turned aside to see, God called unto him out of the midst of the bush, and said, Moses, Moses. And he said, here am I. (Exodus 3:2–4)

The wisdom of Moses is evident in His obedience to the call of God by saying, "Here am I".

We learned previously that the wisdom of God means obedience to the heavenly vision or the call of God. Today, God has been calling many men and women to salvation. He has been calling many unto sanctification and holiness of life, but some have blinded their eyes with the activities and the pleasures of this world. Such people are not wise.

However, in the case of Moses, it was not so.

He obeyed the Lord and took the mantle of God to rescue his people from the hands of Pharaoh in Egypt by the demonstrations of the various wonders of God before Pharaoh and all the children of Israel in the land of Egypt. Moreover, Moses did not end his ministry after delivering the people of God from the hands of Pharaoh in Egypt; rather, he demonstrated another level of God's wisdom by maintaining a consistent walk with the Lord. Our previous studies tell us that *wisdom* means maintaining a consistent walk with the Lord God. How do we know Moses lived and maintained a consistent walk with the Lord?

Throughout the entire Pentateuch, from the time God delivered His people from the hands of Pharaoh in Egypt to the end of his life on earth, Moses maintained a constant obedience to the Lord. He always did exactly what God commanded him as recorded in his books.

In chapter 40, verse 6, of his second book, which is called Exodus, the Word of God tells us that from the time God showed the pattern of the building of the tabernacle unto Moses on the mount to the time the tabernacle was dedicated to the Lord before all the children of Israel, Moses, the servant of the Lord, did "according to all that the Lord commanded him, so did he" (Exodus 40:20).

Moses did not deny the Lord when he received the call. He rather denied himself and embraced the calling and the heavenly vision. The Bible tells us that Moses was a very learned person. He was learned in all the customs and the traditions of the land of Egypt. He was knowledgeable in all the doctrines and activities of Egypt, but he never depended on any of his experience, skills, or knowledge in dealing with the Israelites. He completely depended on God and His presence in his dealings with the people of Israel.

He totally obeyed and relied on God to the extent that he declared that he was not ready to lead the people of Israel if the Lord withheld his presence from among His people. He was an example of a wise leader who demonstrated true obedience to the heavenly vision and calling.

Joshua and Caleb

The lifestyle of Joshua and Caleb is a great demonstration of godly wisdom. These two biblical characters lived a godly lifestyle throughout their lifetimes. When God through His servant Moses called them to be part of those who were chosen to first see the promised land, they did not disobey God and his servant Moses. They spied the land and brought back a good report to Moses the prophet.

Moreover, they not only obeyed the Lord, they also inspired the people of God to serve the Lord. When all the spies returned from surveying the promised land, Joshua and Caleb were the only two servants who encouraged the people and inspired them to keep pressing on to take hold of their possession. The Bible says in Numbers 13:30, "And Caleb stilled the people before Moses, and said, let us go up at once, and possess it; for we are well able to overcome it."

This is great manifestation of a godly wisdom. The word *wisdom,* as we understand from the previous chapters, implies inspiring others to serve and remain in the Lord. Joshua and Caleb did exactly what it means to possess God-given wisdom. Their encouragement went a long way to please the Almighty God in such a way that it really and truly pleased the Lord to forgo his servant Moses when he disobeyed and took only Joshua and Caleb to the promised land.

To crown it all, Joshua and Caleb maintained a consistent walk with the Lord. They followed the Lord fully with all their hearts and everything within them. They walked before the Lord with a sincere heart and mind. They gave all their best to the Lord without any reservation. Even in their old age, they still served the Lord and did much for His kingdom.

What are you doing for the Lord, my dear reader? What legacy are you leaving on this earth for the kingdom of God? What are you doing to add to your crown when you get to the other side of life? The time is now; start doing something for the Lord that nobody has ever done. Bring out your potentials as a child of God. Make yourself available for the Lord, and He will use you greatly for His purpose.

Joseph

Joseph was the son of Isaac and the grandfather of Abraham, the father of all nations. Joseph happens to be the only patriarch who was able to escape the temptation of sexual immorality among all those who faced such temptations.

The wisdom of Joseph is seen in his faithfulness to God throughout his lifetime. He grew up in trust for God. He lived in fear of God as if he were in His very immediate presence. His entire life was controlled by the fear of God. Because of this, he never did anything evil against the Lord. Even when his brothers hated him and sold him into slavery, he held no bitterness against them. When he was sent to prison because of his refusal to sleep with his master's wife, he never tried to defend himself. He put all his trust in the Lord.

He made up his mind to please God in all his endeavors. He acknowledged God in all his ways.

He was one of the few wise men who dedicated his entire life to serving the Lord. He maintained a consistent relationship and fellowship with the Almighty God.

There is no record in the Bible of Joseph sinning or doing evil against his God. No wonder the presence of the Lord was always with him in all the places he found himself. The Bible says in Genesis 39:2, "And the Lord was with Joseph, and he was a prosperous man; and he was in the house of his master the Egyptian."

The Lord did not leave Joseph when he was cast into prison. In fact, God went before him into the prison. The abiding presence of the Almighty God continued with Joseph all the days of his life. In the same chapter, verse 21, the Bible says, "But the Lord was with Joseph, and shewed him mercy, and gave him favor in the sight of the keeper of the prison." Moreover, the Lord was not only with Joseph in the prison, he also gave him favor in the sight of the keeper of the prisoners.

God is always with the wise, always by their

side. He never leaves them alone. He shields and protects them, as well as ensures their progress and promotion in life. He has their real, eternal well-being in mind.

This is the time for you too to seek Jesus. Today is your opportunity to follow godly wisdom and pursue pure understanding.

King David

David was the son of Jesse from the tribe of Judah. The Lord God in His sovereign power and might chose David as the man after His own heart to lead His people. When God called David to lead His people, he perfectly obeyed the Lord and responded to the call. Even though David was young at that time, he did not despise himself or make excuses to disobey the Lord. He foresaw the glory of God upon his life from far off and pursued that with a pure and perfect heart before the Lord.

He walked with the Lord and spent all his years in doing that which pleased Him. His obedience to

God to lead His people is a great example of godly wisdom.

Godly wisdom is a call to obedience and faithfulness to God and His Word. It is a call to live a spotless and blameless life before God and humankind. It is a call to develop a clear conscience regarding God and humankind. It's simply a call to spend the rest of your life in view of eternity. David, the servant of the Lord, knew all these and devoted his time to them.

King Solomon

When David died, God appointed his son Solomon to reign in his stead. Solomon the king began to reign in fear of the Lord. He went in the way of the Lord just as his father David had. His sacrifice to God attracted the presence of God into his life. God, the all-knowing king, was moved by Solomon's actions, and in recognition of the covenant he made with David, His servant, he granted heavenly wisdom to Solomon upon his request. God made him the wisest king ever in the history of the world. The Bible tells us,

> And God gave Solomon wisdom and understanding exceedingly much, and largeness of heart, even as the sand that is on the seashore. And Solomon's wisdom excelled the wisdom of all the children of the east country, and all the wisdom of Egypt. For he was wiser than all men; than Ethan the Ezrahite, and Heman, and Chalcol, and Darda, the sons of Mahol: and his fame was in all nations round about. And he spake three thousand proverbs: and his songs were a thousand and five. And he spake of trees, from the cedar tree that is in Lebanon even unto the hyssop that springeth out of the wall: he spake also of beasts, and of fowl, and of creeping things, and of fishes. And there came of all people to hear the Wisdom of Solomon, from all kings of the earth,

which had heard of his wisdom. (1 Kings 4:29–34)

King Solomon then began to walk and live in the wisdom of the Lord. He demonstrated that wisdom to all the people who were in his realm. He executed judgment through the leading of the Spirit of God. In other words, he allowed the Spirit of God to judge the people. He projected God above and beyond all his plans. He allowed God to lead the people as he followed.

Even though God gave him riches and honor, he served God above all those riches. He did not serve the money, but he served God with the money. He used the riches of his kingdom to develop the kingdom of God, including building a magnificent temple for the Lord. The Bible says, "Then spake Solomon, The LORD said that he would dwell in the thick darkness. I have surely built thee an house to dwell in, a settled place for thee to abide in forever" (1 Kings 8:12–13 KJV). Solomon's wisdom got him all the riches in the world, but he put the Lord God first, before riches, and the Lord put riches in front of Solomon.

Even though Solomon later diverted from the way of the Lord to serve other gods as a result of his marriages to many wives, he realized that nothing in this world could be compared to the wisdom of God. He discovered that all things in this world are vanity of vanities.

My dear reader, King Solomon is no longer here. It's your turn to demonstrate the wisdom for the world to see. This is the time to shine as the light of this world for the kings and the subjects of this world to know and understand the need to serve our God. Do not give up. God is up to something spectacular in your life. He is about to use you to do what nobody has ever done on the face of this earth. Keep trusting and living in His wisdom. Rely only on Jesus, the giver and the source of all godly and pure wisdom.

Elijah

Elijah, the Tishbite, was a prophet of God from the inhabitants of Gilead. How did he demonstrate the wisdom of God in the sight of the children of Israel? Elijah demonstrated God's wisdom by inspiring the people of Israel to understand that they were serving a dead god and that the only true Lord was and is the God of Abraham, the God of Isaac, and the God of Jacob.

When Ahab became king of Israel, he did more evil in the sight of the Lord than all the kings of Israel before him. He not only turned himself aside to worship Baal, he also led the entire nation of Israel to do the same. People who refused to worship Baal were persecuted or driven out of the country, and any true prophet of God who could be found at that time was put to death. This made the people of Israel forget God completely.

Suddenly, one day, the king heard a voice burst forth like a thunderclap, and there stood before him Elijah the prophet of God, saying, "As the Lord God of Israel liveth, before whom I stand, there shall not be dew nor rain these years, but according to my word" (1 Kings 17:1b). Elijah uttered this warning to Ahab and the entire nation of Israel that hunger was at hand.

He was going to show Israel that they were serving a dead god and that only the Lord could send rain. For three years, there was no rain in the land of Israel; the grass disappeared from the hills, the cattle became lin and thin, and nothing grew in the farmers' fields. Day by day the people had less to eat. When Ahab realized the intensity of the famine in the land of Israel, he sent out people to search for the prophet Elijah, but their search yielded no results.

The Bible then tells us that "the word of the Lord came to Elijah in the third year saying, Go, shew thyself unto Ahab; and I will send rain upon the earth" (1 Kings 18:1). He called Israel back to repentance and faith in God by initiating a contest on Mount Carmel. The results of this contest proved to the whole nation of Israel that they were serving a dead god—a god that could neither hear nor speak, an ordinary object that could not be equated to even an animal. I pray the Lord will make you another Elijah in Jesus's mighty name. Stay with the Lord and trust in Him as the only wise God.

Elijah was able to speak the mind of God to the entire nation of Israel even in the presence of Ahab the king. Godly wisdom demands prompt obedience to God without the fear of man or any living soul.

Elisha

Elisha was the son of Shaphat of Abel-meholah. He was anointed by God through the prophet Elijah to take his place prior to his departure, according to 1 Kings 19:16. The hand of the Lord upon the life of Elisha became great and mighty. He received a double portion of Elijah's anointing, which led him to accomplish more than his master Elijah.

God called Elisha to represent His servant Elijah, the prophet, in the land of Israel to be a light during the dark period of that nation. Elisha obeyed God and followed his master Elijah everywhere he went until God took Elijah away by chariots of fire.

Elisha's obedience to God and to Elijah signifies a great demonstration of godly wisdom. It has been declared to us in the previous chapters that godly wisdom has to do with obedience to the heavenly vision. Elisha obeyed the call of God by leaving the oxen that he was farming with and running after Elijah.

Moreover, not only did Elisha obey God and his master, he also maintained a consistent walk with both. He did not allow discouragement from the sons of the prophets and even from his own master to break his connection with God and with his master.

Come with me to 2 Kings 2:1–12, where the Bible says,

> And it came to pass, when the Lord
> would take up Elijah into heaven by a
> whirlwind, that Elijah went with Elisha
> from Gilgal. And Elijah said unto Elisha,
> Tarry here; I pray thee; for the Lord hath

sent me to Beth-el. And Elisha said unto him, As the Lord liveth, and as thy soul liveth, I will not leave thee. So they went down to Beth-el. And the sons of the prophets that were at Beth-el came forth to Elisha, and said unto him, Knowest thou that the Lord will take away thy master from thy head to day? And he said, Yea, I know it; hold ye your peace. And Elijah said unto him, Elisha, tarry here, I pray thee; for the Lord hath sent me to Jericho. And he said, As the Lord liveth, and as thy soul liveth, I will not leave thee. So, they came to Jericho. And the sons of the prophets that were at Jericho came to Elisha, and said unto him, Knowest thou that the Lord will take away thy master from thy head to day? And he answered, Yea, I know it; hold ye your peace. And Elijah said unto him, Tarry, I pray thee, here; for the Lord hath sent me to Jordan. And he said, As the Lord liveth, and as thy soul liveth, I will not leave thee. And they two went on. And fifty men of the sons of the prophets went and stood to view afar off: and they two stood by Jordan. And Elijah took his mantle, and wrapped it together, and smote the waters, and they were divided hither and thither, so that they two went over on dry ground. And it came to pass, when they were gone over, that Elijah said unto Elisha, ask what I shall do for thee, before I be taken away from thee. And Elisha said, I pray thee, let a double portion of thy spirit be upon me. And he said, thou hast asked a hard thing: nevertheless, if thou see me when I am taken from thee, it shall be so unto thee; but if not, it shall not be so. And it came to pass, as they still went on, and talked, that, behold, there appeared a chariot of fire, and horses of fire, and parted them both asunder; and Elijah went up by a whirlwind into heaven. And Elisha saw it, and he cried, My father, my father, the chariot of Israel, and the horsemen thereof. And he saw him no more: and he took hold of his own clothes and rent them in two pieces. (2 Kings 2:1–12 KJV)

Elisha made up his mind to follow God and his master to the end. This is strong evidence of a wise person. God is seeking people like Elisha in this generation who will take their stand for Him even in this crooked and perverse world. I pray you will make yourself available for God to use you mightily in Jesus's mighty name.

Daniel

Daniel was one of the classical prophets of God who devoted all (not part of) his time to serving the Almighty God. He demonstrated a godly character before the kings of Babylon and all the inhabitants of the earth. Daniel's commitment and obedience to God attracted the presence and the hand of God upon his life.

He became the wisest person, full of the understanding of God, in his own time. He demonstrated this wisdom through his determination and perseverance. He took his stand by making prayers and supplications to God even though an edict had been passed against such actions.

He also demonstrated to the king of Babylon as well as all the inhabitants that were upon the face of the earth that there is only one true God who rules and controls the universe. He also proved to the king and all the magicians and astrologers that there is only one wise God who gives understanding and wisdom to his people. He was ten times better than all the magicians and astrologers in his entire realm. Not only that, he was made the third ruler in the province of Babylon.

The demonstration of the wisdom of God in Daniel reveals that God never leaves those who truly and really depend on Him. He always makes Himself known to them wherever they may find themselves. It shows that He is the living God who sits in heaven and directs the movements and the affairs of men with a heavenly device.

My dear reader, I encourage you and charge you to go forth as the Daniel in your home, in your place of work, in your community, in your country, on your continent, and in your world. The Lord Jesus will make it happen in Jesus's mighty name.

Shadrach, Meshach, and Abednego

These were three Hebrew boys in the land of Babylon who decided to preserve the name of the Lord in the world of their time. They took their stand against the standard of King Nebuchadnezzar and the whole nation of Babylon. They agreed to turn the standard of humankind upside down and brought into subjection the thought and the imagination of King Nebuchadnezzar to the obedience of God through the intervention of our Lord and Savior Jesus Christ. They chose to obey God rather than people. They held onto the ordinance of God that was given to them through His servant Moses, which states, "You shall not have any other God apart from me."

Even though they were eventually thrown into the fiery furnace because of their disobedience to the king's ordinances, the Lord Himself descended into their midst as a deliverer from the hands of King Nebuchadnezzar. Their obedience to God despite the impending punishment of the king brought God Himself down in the likeness of man to save His people.

Not only did it bring deliverance to them, but their obedience to God also made the king of the Babylonians realize the power and the authority of the only wise God, who alone deserves to be worshipped and adored and who alone can change the words of kings and any leader that has ever lived on the face of the earth.

Their total obedience to God led the king to make a decree "that every people, nation, and language, which speak anything amiss against the God of Shadrach, Meshach, and Abednego, shall be cut in pieces, and their houses shall be made a dunghill:

because there is no other God that can deliver after this sort" (Daniel 3:29). If you take your stand as a believer today and obey whatsoever God has commanded you to do, many will come to know the Lord through your obedience in Jesus's mighty name.

How did they demonstrate the wisdom of God? Shadrach, Meshach, and Abednego demonstrated the wisdom of God in the sight of the king of Babylon and all his people by walking in the statutes and the ordinances of God given through His servant Moses. They knew that to be full of the wisdom of God meant walking in the light of the Lord. They realized the foolishness of serving other gods apart from the Almighty God who created and owns all things. Their realization empowered them to take their stand by not bowing down to the golden image the king had set up.

My dear reader, are you walking like these three Hebrew children of God? Are all your dreams and focus set on Christ and Christ alone? Who are you standing for today? What are you standing for, and why are you standing for that? If Christ Jesus is not your focus today, then you have missed the starting point. It means you did not start your life on a solid foundation. You must start building your life on Christ the solid rock. Make Him the pillar, the backbone, and the foundation of your life. It only takes a few minutes to decide to follow Him. He needs your sincere realization of self as a sinner and a strong confession of sins with your mouth. You then have to believe with your heart that He has made all things new in your life through His resurrection from the dead. I pray you will take your stand today in Jesus's mighty name.

Job

Job was one of the wisest servants of God who ever lived on the face of the earth. Why is Job considered to be one of the wisest? He was a servant of God because he feared God and eschewed evil all the days of his life.

He knew by the inspiration of the Holy Spirit that the fear of the Lord is the beginning of divine wisdom. Therefore, he took it upon himself to live in the fear of the Lord. He lived his life as if he were in the immediate presence of the Almighty God. When God allowed the enemy to tempt and test him, he never sinned against God or humankind. He never allowed those trials to shape his focus and change his mindset about God. He took his stand. He simply maintained a consistent walk with God during various troubles.

He made God his all in all. He projected God above wealth and life. He trusted in God above and beyond friends and foes. I pray you too will take your stand. You will not allow the things in this world to take you away from Christ and take Christ away from you. I pray the Lord will make you wise in Jesus's mighty name.

Ruth

Ruth is considered to be one of the wisest women who ever lived. Why is Ruth considered to be wise? How did she demonstrate her godly wisdom?

Ruth was from the land of Moab and a daughter

in law to Naomi, whose husband, Elimelech, had died and left her with two sons. Ruth married one of Naomi's sons, but he also died, leaving Ruth alone.

After the death of Ruth's husband, Ruth made a wise decision to follow her mother-in-law despite Naomi's pressure and discouragement. Ruth made up her mind to follow Naomi everywhere she might go.

Now, the most significant part of Ruth's decision to follow Naomi was the fact that she was taking her stand to follow the God of Naomi. According to Ruth 1:16,

> And Ruth said, Entreat me not to leave thee, or to return from following after thee: for whither thou goest, I will go; and where thou lodgest, I will lodge: thy people shall be my people, and thy God my God: Where thou diest, will I die, and there will I be buried: the Lord do so to me, and more also, if ought but death part thee and me. (Ruth 1:16–17 KJV)

Ruth left her father, her mother, and her native land to cleave to Naomi and her God. Her decision to follow the Almighty God changed her life story entirely. The God of Naomi also blessed her and made her the mother of all mothers, to whom the lineage of our Lord and Savior Jesus Christ can be traced today. It is indeed wise to decide to follow Christ Jesus. I don't know what you may be going through now, but I want to encourage you with the knowledge that, regardless of the situation, if you can cleave to Jesus, your entire life and everything about you will change from today in Jesus's mighty name. As He lifted Ruth from the dust and placed her among the prominent, so will the Almighty God do for you and your family in Jesus's mighty name. Like Ruth, decide today to cleave unto Jesus, the life changer, and He will change your life, your family, and your ministry in Jesus's mighty name.

Jesus

Jesus, the Savior of this world, is the wisest person who has ever lived and is still living and reigning in the hearts of all those who believe in Him through His suffering death and glorious resurrection. No one can understand the depth of His wisdom.

His birth was prophesied in wisdom by a wise angel. He was born to a wise woman named Mary through the inspiration of the Spirit of wisdom. He was brought up and grown in wisdom. He ministered wisdom and taught in wisdom. He suffered in wisdom and died as a result of His wisdom. He resurrected in wisdom and glorified the all-wise God, the omnipotent, omnipresent, and the ever-living creator.

He is simply wisdom personified. He is wise in deeds, words, and all things. He is full of wisdom. Call on Him if you are confused and do not know what to do. Meditate in His Word when you are about to make major and minor decisions in life. Rely on His spoken word whenever you feel rejected and dejected. Moreover, when you carefully examine the acronym of the word *wisdom*, it is truly clear that Jesus Himself is the light of the world.

- **W:** Jesus **walked** in the light of the world. As a light, He demonstrated to His disciples and the generations to come how they could also walk in the light of the world. He lived a sinless life in a sinful world. He shines as the light to expel every deed of darkness. He is the light that shines to show the way that leads to life eternal.

- **I:** He **inspired** His disciples and others to walk in the light and in the way of the Lord. In the gospel according to Matthew, the Bible tells us that Jesus inspired His disciples to "let their light shine before all men, that they may see their good deeds and glorify the father which is in heaven" (5:16). Jesus spent all His life on earth preaching and inspiring others to come to the kingdom of God. No one could ever inspire more than Jesus. In fact, He is the source of all inspirations. He inspires, His words inspire, His actions inspire, everything about Him and around Him inspires. Read and meditate in His Word daily, and your heart and your life will be full of inspirations.

- **S**: In the process of inspiring His disciples and others, Jesus **served** them to the point of washing their feet. He served both God and humans with sincerity of heart without any reservations. Even though He is the Messiah, he demonstrated a messianic servanthood, forsaking His Lordship and glory and taking the place of a servant. No leader has been able to attain the position of Jesus. No one has been able to reach the utmost height that Jesus reached; yet he did not count Himself worthy to be a master. He was and is still the godliest man who ever lived, yet He did not count Himself worthy to be called good (Mark 10:18).

- **D**: We have previously learned that wisdom also means **doing the will** of the Father who is in heaven. Jesus declared plainly to His parents, His disciples, and all those who heard Him that He came to do the will of the Father who is in heaven. He delighted in doing God's will more than He enjoyed His necessary food. In the gospel according to St. John, the Bible says, "Jesus saith unto them, my meat is to do the will of him that sent me, and to finish his work" (4:34). He demonstrated heavenly wisdom by doing the will of God. He spent all His years on earth as an ambassador of His father. Seek Him and you shall find wisdom.

The Eleven Apostles

The eleven apostles of our Lord and Savior Jesus Christ truly demonstrated godly wisdom during and after the ministry of Jesus Christ. They were more than eleven in number, but for the sake of the subject of godly wisdom, we are mostly interested in the eleven. The reason is that Judas Iscariot, who happened to be the twelfth apostle, did not demonstrate any godly wisdom from the time he was called to the time he betrayed the only begotten son of God. He could be described as the most foolish apostle. For this reason, he cannot be added to the list of the wise apostles.

Now, coming back to the eleven apostles of Christ, it is recorded in the scriptures that they turned their own world upside down with the preaching of the gospel. When Jesus called them to follow Him, none of them refused the calling. They all responded to the call with readiness to serve.

When Peter was called, he forsook his boat and all he had to follow Christ. When the call came to John the Beloved, he simply obeyed. Matthew left his profession as a tax collector and followed Jesus. Others left their fathers and followed Jesus. The eleven apostles not only obeyed the call of God; they followed the footsteps of Christ fully. They maintained a consistent walk with the Lord Jesus Christ, not fearing the shame and the despising people. They went everywhere with the boldness of the Spirit of God declaring that Jesus was the Christ. The threats of the scribes and the Pharisees, as well as the religious leaders, could not stop them from proclaiming the only Savior to the world. They kept on pursuing the heavenly goal of serving the master to the very end.

Mary Magdalene

The Bible tells us that Mary Magdalene is the woman from whom Jesus cast out seven evil spirits. After her deliverance, she continued walking with the Lord. She did not go back to the world. She demonstrated godly wisdom by giving all her best to the Master. She did not consider the value of what she was going to give to the Lord Jesus, but she wholeheartedly and unreservedly broke open the alabaster jar of ointment and poured it on the hair of Christ.

Not only did she give all she had to Christ, she also continued serving the Lord fully. In other words, she maintained a consistent walk with the Lord. She held onto the words Jesus said before His crucifixion, that he would die and be buried but in three days would come back to life. She never doubted His words.

Mary Magdalene continued with Lord Jesus even

after His death. She rose early in the morning and went to the sepulchre (tomb) of Christ to seek Him. No wonder she was the only living soul upon the earth who first saw Christ after His resurrection, before Jesus ascended to meet with the Father in heaven.

She sought the Lord and found him. She was indeed wise.

Paul the Apostle

Paul, who was formerly known as Saul of Tarsus, was called to be an apostle, a servant, and a witness of our Lord Jesus Christ. Before his calling, the Bible says he was an injurious man who did more harm to Christianity than any man that had ever lived before him. The scriptures describe his old, sinful life as one of foolishness and lacking wisdom in the sight of Lord.

However, when the Lord Jesus appeared to him on his way to Damascus to execute his assignment of persecuting believers who were standing for the Lord at that time, his life underwent a total transformation. His old life of foolishness changed to a new life of wisdom. His old life as a servant and slave to sin changed to one of a new man with freedom from sins, a witness of the gospel, and a servant of our Lord Jesus Christ.

As an apostle of Christ, he was willing to take the gospel message across the world despite the challenges and circumstances. He was not moved by the dangers and the challenges associated with taking the gospel message to many nations. He was ready to sacrifice his very life for the gospel's sake. We are told in the book of the Acts of the Apostles that when other believers tried to discourage Paul from embarking on his missionary journey to Jerusalem—as a result of one prophet named Agabus's saying that the Holy Ghost had given him a word that the Jews in Jerusalem would bind Paul and deliver him into the hands of the Gentiles— "Then Paul answered, What mean ye to weep and to break mine heart? for I am ready not to be bound only, but also to die at Jerusalem for the name of the Lord Jesus" (Acts 21:13). Moreover, as a servant of

Christ, he was ready to do the master's command with eagerness. As a witness, he was bound to preach the saving gospel of the Lord Jesus Christ.

These things characterized the life and the ministry of Paul the apostle. He was characteristically consumed with passion for the heavenly vision, as he declared before King Agrippa in Acts 26:16–19:

> But rise, and stand upon thy feet: for I have appeared unto thee for this purpose, to make thee a minister and a witness both of these things which thou hast seen, and of those things in the which I will appear unto thee; Delivering thee from the people, and from the Gentiles, unto whom now I send thee, To open their eyes, and to turn them from darkness to light, and from the power of Satan unto God, that they may receive forgiveness of sins, and inheritance among them which are sanctified by faith that is in me. Whereupon, O king Agrippa, I was not

disobedient unto the heavenly vision. (Acts 26:16–19 KJV)

When the call of God came upon him, he did not harden his heart, but he faithfully obeyed the heavenly calling as a light to the Gentiles. His response to King Agrippa in Acts 26:19 attests to this: "Whereupon, O king Agrippa, I was not disobedient unto the heavenly vision" (KJV). His obedience to the heavenly vision makes him one of the wisest apostles.

Paul not only obeyed the calling of God, he also understood that the call to follow Christ is a call to suffer for the sake of the gospel. Therefore he did not allow the reactions and the actions of the religious leaders to hinder him from fulfilling his call. He rather took it upon himself to inspire others to walk and remain in the light of the Lord. Godly wisdom is all about inspiring others to remain in the Lord. Every wise man is required to bring others out of darkness into the light of Christ. Paul the apostle was such a man in his time.

He preached the gospel message in every place

he found himself. He made the preaching of the gospel his daily duty. He even said, "Woe unto me if I preach not the gospel" (1 Corinthians 9:16). He preached to more souls than he had persecuted. He won more souls for Christ than he had wiped out. He inspired more souls in Christ than he had despised. He encouraged more souls in Christ than he had discouraged. He did more for Christ than he took from Christ.

Moreover, Paul the apostle is also known to be one of the biblical characters who served God faithfully to the very end. He did not allow his past life to stop him from serving the Lord. He focused all his attention on the one who had called him—Jesus. He was indeed a wise master builder who laid the foundation of genuine repentance and true holiness for the entire body of Christ (1 Corinthians 3:10).

Throughout his ministry, he chose God above everything he had in life. He suffered persecution but never gave up. He was afflicted to the point of death, but he still maintained a consistent walk with the Lord.

The Importance of
Possessing God-
Give Wisdom

It has become crucial, due to the rampant deception of the enemy, for every child of God in this generation to desire to be wise. King Solomon, in his own time, displayed the wisdom of God to the nation. The Bible tells us that there was no one like him, neither can there be anyone like him in wisdom and in might. He took his time to write the book of Proverbs and explained to us the significance of godly wisdom.

In chapter 8 of Proverbs, he makes it clear in verse 2 that wisdom sets us above others. It places us in high places, just like Joseph, who was lifted from the dungeon to the position of prime minister because of His wisdom (Genesis 37–50).

Daniel too displayed divine wisdom in the province of Babylon, and through that, he was ten times better than all of the magicians and astrologers who were in the realm. Not only that, he was made the third ruler in the province of Babylon (Daniel 5:29).

Divine wisdom enables one to speak right things at the right time, according to Proverbs 8:7–9. We desire God's wisdom because it is more precious than worldly riches and wealth, as discussed in verse 11. Money, wealth, and worldly possessions can never compare to the wisdom of God. Earthly acquisitions and achievements can never be equated with what the wisdom of God can give. It is simply incomparable to all the riches and wealth in this world.

Verse 1 states that wisdom makes it possible to rule over oneself as well as one's home, one's community, and the entire nation. In other words, people with godly wisdom have self-control and self-discipline. Such people always exercise authority over their entire households without fear or favor. They use the Word of God to rule their own houses. The demonstration of their godly wisdom positively influences their community and the entire world.

Verse 20 states that wisdom helps people execute

righteous judgment without fear or favor. It does not matter how familiar people are with the laws and the constitution governing a country or nation. If they lack God's wisdom, such knowledge of the law is useless and senseless. Any leader, ruler, or governor who really wants to excel and exceed the expectations of the people under his or her leadership must possess godly wisdom.

Above all, it is crucial for every believer to seek godly wisdom because Christ Jesus Himself is wisdom personified. He is the originator and the wisdom itself. From verse 22 through verse 31, the Bible affirms that Christ is the wisdom of God:

> The Lord possessed me in the beginning of his way, before his works of old. I was set up from everlasting, from the beginning, or ever the earth was. When there were no depths, I was brought forth, when there were no fountains abounding with water. Before the mountains were settled, before the hills was I brought forth: while yet he had

not made the earth, nor the fields, nor the highest part of the dust of the world. When he prepared the heavens, I was there: when he set a compass upon the face of the depth: When he established the clouds above: when he strengthened the fountains of the deep: When he gave to the sea his decree, that the waters should not pass his commandment: when he appointed the foundations of the earth: Then I was by him, as one brought up with him: and I was daily his delight, rejoicing always before him; Rejoicing in the habitable part of his earth; and my delights were with the sons of men. (Proverbs 8:22–31 KJV).

The above verses of Scriptures not only reveal Christ as the wisdom of God, they also teach us that whoever has Christ has godly wisdom. If one does not have Christ, then such a person cannot be called wise. You can be called a wise man or woman in the sight of men, but you are the opposite in the sight of God if you do not have Jesus as your Lord and Savior. It does not really matter how far people go in education and training, how successful they may think they are, or what talents and skills they may acquire and work with. If Christ Jesus is absent in their lives, they are not wise people.

The three wise men who—despite all their knowledge, experience, and intelligence in their endeavors—set aside the time to search for Christ when they saw His star in the East teach us a lot of lessons about the wisdom of God. It tells us that no one, including professors, doctors, teachers, bankers, accountants, soldiers, police officers, kings and queens, rich and poor, small and great, young and old, men and women, is exempt from seeking and searching for Christ, who is the most intelligent and wisest man who ever lived.

How Can One Receive
God's Wisdom?

The sacred scripture has made it as clear as crystal that divine and godly wisdom begins with the fear of God. "The fear of the Lord is the beginning of wisdom" (Proverbs 9:10a). This tells us that no man or woman can possess godly wisdom without the fear of God. The fear of God, therefore, becomes the basic qualification for all those who really and truly desire to be wise not in their own sight but that of the Lord.

What does it really mean to fear the Lord? First, to fear the Lord simply means obeying and doing the will of God as if you are in the very immediate presence of the Almighty God. Second, it means projecting God above any other thing in your life. It means continuously walking and living in the consciousness of the Almighty God all the time.

People who fear God are always ready to do His will at all costs. They are ready to lose their belongings and possessions for the sake of the kingdom of God. They are ever ready to die and lose their lives on this earth because of Jesus. They never get tired of serving the Lord. They are always ready at the service of the Lord and fears nothing but God.

Why is it so important to possess fear of God to have godly wisdom? First, it is revealed in the Holy Bible that the fear of the Lord is the beginning of wisdom. When people fear the Lord, they become wise in the sight of the Lord. Second, God is the giver of godly wisdom, so anyone who desires to be wise in His sight must first fear Him.

When you compare Proverbs 9:10a to James 1:5, it will give you clear understanding of those who qualify to receive God's wisdom. King Solomon, by inspiration of the Holy Spirit, gave us what is known to be the foundation of wisdom. James the apostle, in his epistle, also revealed to us the promise of divine wisdom in James 1:5.

Simply put, to be able to access the promise of

the wisdom of God revealed in this epistle, one must go back to the foundation that is already given in Proverbs 9:10.That is the fear of God.

If you carefully examine James 1:5, which says, "If any of you lack wisdom, let him ask of God, that giveth to all men liberally, and upbraideth not; and it shall be given him," you may see that the phrase "if any of you" does not necessarily apply to all people or any person literally. It takes off the veil and reveals the truth that fear of God is crucial in the desire to possess the wisdom of God.

When you look at the context of James's epistle, it is obvious that he was talking to believers who had been truly washed and purged from all sins. He was talking to those who had already come to the saving knowledge of our Lord and Savior Jesus Christ. He was addressing those who fear the Lord.

In verse 1 of the same chapter, James refers to the readers as *brethren*, which implies believers in that context. In verse 3, he adds to the point by saying, "Knowing this, that the trying of your faith worketh patience." The phrase "your faith" speaks to us about people who have believed in Jesus Christ as their Lord and Savior.

All these add to the fact that it is obvious that God does not give His wisdom to sinners or to those who are outside the sheepfold. He gives it to those who are His children.

There is only one sure way sinners can gain an opportunity to request the wisdom of God. They must be born again before thinking of acquiring godly wisdom from the Lord. They must acknowledge their sinful state and confess those sins to God. They must then believe with sincerity of heart that the blood of Jesus alone is enough to wash all their sins away and make them new creatures. After this is done, then there is an assurance of salvation that will eventually energize them to ask God for anything they may desire according to His will, including wisdom.

Are you ready for the godly wisdom that God is ready to give to you free of charge? Sincerely believe in Him as the only giver of godly wisdom. Then call on Him with faith, and He will surely answer you in Jesus's mighty name.

Living and Laboring in His Wisdom Till His Return

Our Lord and Savior Jesus applied His wisdom to save souls. He did all He could with His power to make sure that all those with whom He interacted experienced the gift of the Father to the world. Even in His encounter with the controversial Pharisees and the Sadducees, who were downright evil and trying to discredit Him and to condemn, contradict, and destroy His entire ministry, He applied His wisdom to point them to the very basic and essential experience in ministry, which is salvation.

For instance, when He encountered the woman who had been caught in adultery, instead of supporting their condemnation, He diverted the attention on the woman to the people intending to stone her, telling them that their own salvation should be the utmost priority in their lives. Christ's wise actions, His wise approach, and His wise answer to the Pharisees and the Sadducees convicted even the schemers.

My dear reader, what are you using your wisdom for? Are you using it to expand your ministerial assignment in the kingdom, or you are using your wisdom to deceive your church members? Many ministers today are selling the gospel of Christ to some of those under their authority.

8

Conclusion

There is no doubt that the wisdom of this world (cunning, craftiness, selfishness, sensuality, fleshly dispositions, and carnality) is counted as foolishness by God. Satan, the god of this world, rules the worldly system. But true wisdom is divine and only comes from the Creator of the heavens and the earth. By this wisdom, He created all things visible and invisible. By this wisdom, He rules and reigns for eternity. By this wisdom, He maintains all things in their courses. By this wisdom, He planned salvation for humankind, and by this wisdom, He will eventually judge the whole of humanity, from Adam to the last person at the end of all things.

One good thing about God is that He wants to share this wisdom with all people who are willing to accept Jesus as Lord and Savior of all their affairs. This possibility is within your reach even today.

Above all, beyond all, going ahead of everything, it is crucial to understand that the term *godly wisdom* can be summed up as an act of rendering an acceptable and reasonable service unto God. To render acceptable service to God means presenting your body as a living sacrifice holy and acceptable to God, according to Paul the apostle by inspiration in his epistle to the Romans (12:1).

It will be of no use if you try to render a service to God when holiness is absent in your life. God does not recognize such service. On this note, it is clear that holiness unto the Lord and godly wisdom move together. They join hand in hand. Without the holiness of God, there is no godly wisdom.

Godly wisdom is a call to obedience and faithfulness to God and His Word. It is a call to live a spotless and blameless life before God and humans. It is a call to develop a clear conscience regarding God and humankind. It's simply a call to spend the rest of your life in view of eternity.

Printed in the United States
By Bookmasters